HennaMan

3/00

1/50

Also by Derrick I. M. Gilbert (a.k.a. D-Knowledge)

CATCH THE FIRE!!!: A CROSS-GENERATIONAL ANTHOLOGY
OF CONTEMPORARY AFRICAN-AMERICAN POETRY
(editor)

HennaMan

Poems by

Derrick I.M. Gilbert

(a.k.a. **D-Knowledge**)

RIVERHEAD BOOKS
New York

Riverhead Books
Published by The Berkley Publishing Group
A division of Penguin Putnam Inc.
375 Hudson Street
New York, New York 10014

"We Wear the Mask," by Paul Laurence Dunbar from *The Collected Poetry of Paul Laurence Dunbar*, Joanne M. Braxton, ed. (Charlottesville: Virginia, 1993). Reprinted with permission of the University Press of Virginia.

Copyright © 2000 by Derrick I. M. Gilbert
Book design by Tiffany Kukec
Cover design by Miguel Santana
Cover art by Shiva Ghodsi and Miguel Santana

First edition: March 2000

The Penguin Putnam Inc. World Wide Web site address is
http://www.penguinputnam.com

Library of Congress Cataloging-in-Publication Data

Gilbert, Derrick I. M.
    HennaMan : poems/by Derrick I.M. Gilbert (a.k.a. D-Knowledge).—1st ed.
        p. cm.
    ISBN 1-57322-809-5
    1. Afro-Americans—Poetry. I. Title: Henna man. II. Title.

PS3557.I3395 H46 2000
811'.54—dc21   99-054644

Printed in the United States of America

10 9 8 7 6 5 4 3 2 1

Contents

Foreword

by Sonia Sanchez

He walked out onto the Apollo stage in New York City, leaned his body on history, poured his tongue into a whirlwind of words and color. He said REMEMBER. And we did. And he grew large, suddenly, like a fire in the wind, and his words burst into flames, igniting us all with sanctified nods of Amen. Brother. Yeah. Brother-man. Tell it like 'tis. Word.

When did this young man called D-Knowledge learn to sail his masculine words on our sequestered memories until our heads jerked back in recognition? How did he pull us from our unremembered youth, our past activism in the midst of these ahistorical times? How do you spell Poet in these pseudo-poetical times?

You spell him Derrick Gilbert, a name given to him by his parents as he walked his young legs on Long Beach. Watching always. Learning from the streets; not particularly interested during his early years in books or things of the intellect. But smart. Brilliant in his watchfulness. Waiting. Incubator style.

You spell him D-KNOWLEDGE, a name given to him by his peers at the University of California, Berkeley, where he began to read two books a week, moving his arms, hands, and eyes on a mission of knowledge as he came out of his incubation, cracking his shell and our skulls in the process. D-Knowledge. Liberating name.

You spell him PH.D. MAN in sociology back at UC Berkeley, where he reads and interprets and analyzes the origins and history of human society. Yeah. 'Cuz is all that.

You spell him AFRICAN-AMERICAN POET MAN on a mission, more interested in challenging and teaching us all with his commentary and humor than hitting skins. You call him Poet. In the Tradition.

Do you remember the first time you were home? At peace with yourself? Yes. Something like a first love. Holier than even that. D-Knowledge was home as he surrounded himself with poets, musicians, and artists from Leimert Park, as he read writers like June Jordan, Amiri Baraka, and Gil Scott-Heron. He knew he was finally home as he began the practiced step of poetry, with its inevitable rhythm and beat. And he followed that ancestral beat home to where words became women and men, where flesh walked upright. Finally. And his poetry asked no favors. Took no prisoners.

And Hamilton Cloud, in 1993, at the NAACP Image Awards Program, saw and heard all that and more. He began talking and negotiating with the young wordsmith who had electrified the audience that night. Hamilton Cloud and Ramon Hervey began the work of bringing this unique poet to a larger audience.

Within months D-Knowledge had a guest appearance in John Singleton's film *Higher Learning*. He wrote a poem for the movie.

Next he appeared in Mario Van Peeble's film *Panther*; then a shot on Arsenio Hall's show that showed the country the power of this young poet's words; he signed with Qwest Records, Quincy Jones's label, to do an album, *All That and a Bag of Words*; and finally he edited *Catch The Fire!!!: A Cross-Generational Anthology of Contemporary African-American Poetry.*

From the impulse of teacher, he has become the name and namer of his poems. And a mighty sound is heard in the land. He cajoles the young to be drug free, gun free, macho free, baby free, nigger free. He asks us to conquer any fear that may hold us back. He asks us to continue to learn and study and read and resist. Resist anything that keeps us from being human.

From the impulse of lover, he implores us to love ourselves, our big and thin lips, our wide and narrow noses, our Black and fair skins, our nappy, curly, and straight hair. He tells us to stay deep and focused on ourselves so we can begin the beginning work of loving ourselves and our people, and then we will be capable of loving others.

From the impulse of poet, he has chosen the voice of the Courageous one. The same voice we all must choose to make this a better world for our children. As poet, he offers himself as a mouthpiece for those who have no mouths. As poet, he tries to reestablish harmony in the world.

His words will put meat on your bones.

Money is all that!

HennaMan

Part 1

Vitiligo

Mask Cracking

I.

When I was in gray-grade school
I was the quickest/fastest kid around
I could out race
Race
I could number-two pencil
Erase my face
And Hannibal Lectorize
A decarbonized copy in its
Scan-troned space
My identity was a multiple choice of
(Fill in the blank)
Bubble confusion
I really wanted a white boy soul transfusion
And I climbed high up the jungle-book gym
To reach this end
When
At about ten
I was called
White Boy
On San Andreas cracked asphalt
(Whose fault?)
By students who looked liked me
But bused to Newcomb Elementary
From a not welcomed reality
My white friends said they came from
A cartoon/cocooned
Place called the ghetto

Articulated with a stuttering staccato
Followed with a
"You know, Derrick . . .
You're not really Black"
With the quickly adapted addendum
"At least you're not like them"
Which became their
National one Black friend anthem:
You're not like them!
You're not like them!
You're not like them!
And
I believed them

II.

Now I lay me down to sleep
I pray the Lord my darkness seeps
If I die before I wake
This skin of Black I hope you take

III.

Third period of ninth grade
Was taught by Mr. Randall
First teacher/pal
To hippie hip me to edible metaphors
And got me listening to the Doors
One Pop-Tart morning
He floored me with a breakfast buffet of verse
But nothing was tempting

Not even the French villanelled toast
Or the Shakespearean-spiced sonnet omelettes
Or the no-fat haiku flakes
Or the not so freshly squeezed rhyme juice . . .
But then arose an aroma that loosened my nasal nuisances
First bite brought first light and a tickling insight
As my taste buds became translucent
With Paul Laurence Dunbar's voice
Making my tongue poetically fluent:

> We wear the mask that grins and
>   lies,
>   It hides our cheeks and shades our
>   eyes,—
>   This debt we pay to human guile,
>   With torn and bleeding hearts we
>   smile,
> And mouth with myriad subtle-
>   ties.

But wait
After a take-five
Minute dictionary break
I realized he said *we*
To say what I thought
Only happened to me and me
(Damn, D)
He even used *our*
To describe what applied to
I and I
Who thought I was the sole soul perplexed racial solo
The singular Ham-curried cursed son
Who wanted to scrape his pigment

With Brillo pads
I and I
Who lied about the lye
On my head
Telling folks an S-curl
Was my real hair—
Totally unaware
There were others
Out there
Ding dong ditching their
Self of self
Trying to be somebody else
But for me
The playground masquerade was finally
Heading toward
Game over
Moreover
I now had a face guard remover
A self-sorrow soother
A ballpoint groover . . .
I had the we-creation of me word
And this ancestrally saged bird
Began aiming his droppings on the page
With Dunbar eagle-humming a new praise:

> But let the world dream otherwise . . .
> While we mesmerize, tantalize
> And whirl our facial clay in the sky;
> We wore the mask!

Kittician Duality

I.

Crystal waves that have never carried me through the days
Simmering sand that has never sizzled my toes
Coconut trees that have never scraped my skin
Spices that have never teased my palate
Peculiar flowers that have never made me giggle
(Or awakened my allergies)
A land I have never touched
But a land that has curiously caressed me
(St. Kitts/St. Kitts)
Home of my father's tobacco
And his father's finger-crafted corn pipe
And my mother's banana-bundled pudding pie
And her mother's deserted recipes
(St. Kitts/St. Kitts)
Brought to this Caribbean shore
Centuries before in corroded chains/in snaggy shackles
In decaying freedom
Forced to cultivate a foreign soil
Challenged to plant home seeds
In an unfamiliar terrain
Propelled to harvest humanity
In a venomous domain
Exquisite in their resourcefulness
In their perseverance
In their nurturing
In their loving
In . . .

(St. Kitts/St. Kitts)
And though
I have never touched this land
It has tenderly rubbed me
Giving me seawater rhythms
Sun-tickled beats
Sounds of Kittician joy
Regenerating my blood
Transfusing history into my veins
Invigorating my existence
Giving me light
Giving me life
My mother's life/my father's life
My sister's life
My ancestrally extended family's life
My life
Line
(St. Kitts/St. Kitts)
And yes
St. Kitts is my home
My multilingual mirror tells me so
My mother's well-digested banana pie lets me know
My father's overweight tobacco puff makes it flow
My grandmother's undeserted legacy ensures it grows
And
My eyelids
Gently
Collapse
And
Finally
I am home
(St. Kitts/St. Kitts)

II.

Mystical sand
Overwhelmed with egomaniacal bodies
Drenched in suntan
Lotion
Standin'/layin'
In gall
Unremorsefully pissin' in the ocean
Savagely skippin' free
Colonizing the sea shore
Enslaving cracked shells
Genocidally torturing the breeze
Only pausin'
To have the "natives"
Massage their personalities
Cuddle their consciousness
Rub their sun-popped flesh
With ultra-violet superiority
And niggerize their hair with
Geographically unspecific
French braids
And
Is this my home?
(St. Kitts)
'Cause the banana pies are spoiled
The tobacco makes me nauseous
Blurs my sanity
And makes me crawl in West Indian Marlboro Country
And my grandmother is a double decade deceased
And is this my home?
(St. Kitts)
'Cause my cousins

Are falling through virtual
Quicksand maze
Catering
Accommodating
Acquiescing to
Sitcom stars' dreams
And I'm still inversely trippin'
Over the French braid thing
And I'm sinking in a worldwide weave
WWW
But no dot
'Cause I've been deceived
And
My eyelids fling open
And
My ears buzz
As an airline attendant
Tosses me a nosebleed-stained pillow
A stressed-out hairy blanket
And with a well-trained smile asks:
"Are you going home?"
And I reply
I thought so . . .
(St. Kitts/St. Kitts)

Resourcefulness

When Michael Jackson
George Benson
Patti LaBelle
Stephanie Mills
And all those others
Got their nose jobs
I wonder what happened
To all the
Leftover meat
'Cause we could probably
Take all that left over meat
Sculpt it into a
Big
Twenty-two-foot-high
Broad
Black
Nose
And take it to Egypt
And place it on the
Sphinx

The Revolution Will Be on the Big Screen

My man Gil Scott-Heron once said:
"You will not be able to stay home, brother
You will not be able to plug in, turn on, and cop out
You will not be able to lose yourself on scag and
skip out for beer during commercial because
The Revolution will not be televised"

Gil Scott may have a point
The Revolution will not be televised
But it will be a major motion picture
The Revolution will not be televised
But the Revolution will be on the big screen.

The Revolution will be a billion-dollar production
Written by John Grisham and directed by Steven Spielberg
The Revolution will star Kevin Costner and Julia Roberts
And they will teach people of color
How to revolt . . . how to rebel . . . how to kill . . . and how to scream
The Revolution will be on the big screen.

The Revolution will have one Latino extra (Edward James Olmos)
Playin' a thief
One Asian extra (Jackie Chan)
Playin' an eighth-degree cook
And one Native American extra
Played by a moccasin-wearing Bruce Willis
Runnin' down Florence and Normandie

Yellin' "yeepeekayyay!"
The Revolution will be on the big screen.

The Revolution will have two Black supporting actors
One: Morgan Freeman
'Cause Daisy's been resurrected
And she needs a ride back down South
Two: Denzel Washington
Who will be killed in the first three minutes
By Kevin Costner
For looking at Julia Roberts
For more than four seconds
While Kevin Costner will have a picture of Whitney Houston
Burnin' in his wallet
The Revolution will be on the big screen.

The Revolution will be coming soon to a theater near you
And will get two thumbs-up from Siskel and Ebert
And will make more many than *Jurassic Park* and *E.T.*
The Revolution will cost $8.50 to see or $5.50 if you got a student ID
The Revolution will go good with popcorn, bonbons, and licorice
The Revolution will be on the big screen.

The Revolution will have a multiplatinum sound track
With subversive songs sung by
Marilyn Manson, Madonna, and the Spice Girls
The Revolution will be advertised on billboards, buses, Web sites, T-shirts
And with Hitler's lost testicle reincarnated as a Chihuahua
Leading the coup for Taco Bell
"*Viva la revolución,* suckers"
The Revolution will be on the big screen.

The Revolution will be distributed internationally

The Revolution will be seen in Cuba, Croatia, and Haiti
The Revolution will be on the big screen.

The Revolution will have a sequel
The Revolution will have a part III
The Revolution will be too large for TV
Too large for the little screen
("It's going to be huge, man")
The Revolution will not be televised
Will not be televised/Not be televised
But
The Revolution will be on the big screen.

Devil's Advocate

It was 6:58 on the Santa Monica Promenade and I had just concluded an intellectually invigorating date . . . But it was early and I knew I could discover another fate . . . So I paced the boredom walk in shoes that were more cute than comfortable . . . Until I stopped in a homogenized sports bar to catch the Lake Show—and not Ricki but the Los Angeles Lakes . . . But damn . . . the Miami Heat were in a blaze . . . Even though swift/trick-handed Van Nexel was performing magic that reminded Riley of his dyslexic Johnson daze . . . But—still—my team was in a malaise . . . And I wasn't going to witness their first losing phase . . .

So I decided to head back to the crib . . . Find my bed and get in it . . . When a billboard possessed me . . . The letters were neon-lit and read: *Devil's Advocate/Devil's Advocate* . . . And I really wanted to see this flick . . . And it was showing in a country minute . . . So I made an ATM debit and—oh well—bought an eight-dollar ticket . . .

But peep . . . There was only 1 body occupying the cinematic seats . . . And when he went to pee . . . I almost felt lonely . . . So I chose the most middle/theatrical spot so that the THX speakers would keep me company—Then I sat down . . . Positioned my spine in my ephemeral throne . . . And nonchalantly dangled my right limb over the cushioned pew in front of me . . . And chilled in the comfort zone . . . Periodically watching miscellaneous shadows stumble in to find a similar serenity . . . When two long-haired ivory silhouettes who reminded me of my Berkeley school daze hovered over my tranquillity . . .

And—with great equanimity—the taller of the two says: Do you mind???

I play dim-witted and say: Mind what???

He say: Mind moving your leg . . .

I say: Look at this big ol' theater . . . You can sit anywhere!!!

The unspoken/shorter one say: It's a center-of-gravity thing, dude.

I say: Well . . . center your gravity somewhere else, dude.

Attitude dude say: We can sit wherever we want . . . and this is it!!!

Prompted by his anal tone, I say: You gota problem?

He say: Yeah . . . you're my problem.

I rise and say: So what you gonna do . . .
    (*But I give the statement a little profane vernacular push . . .*)
    MUTHA—!

(*I sense the sparse crowd observing the scene as they sniff testoster-one sautéing and ego baking*)

He say: I'm not going to do anything—'cause I don't believe in violence like you.

I say: Violence???

He instinctively knows I'm asking a question and says: Yeah, man, violence that's all you seem to know.

Now I'm tripping . . . 'Cause he really thinks I'm gonna steal on him . . . I deduce that he doesn't know I'm a laid-back kinda cat who would rather throw blows with lyrical dexterity . . . Block his futile attacks with semantical swiftness and strategic polysyllables . . . And finally knock him out with Sankofa passion expressed with hypo-animated inflections and intonations . . . But . . . quite honestly . . . his pompous accusations challenged my peaceful Ghandian stance—'Cause I wanted to gag him with overly salted popcorn . . . But to elude this calm breakdown . . . I moved one seat over and propped my foot on a new cushion . . .

And he say: Now I gotta look at your big/ugly shoe.

I say: What. . . . bleep/bleep/bleep!
(My eloquence and word diversity are suspended for the moment)

He say: You know . . . You don't have to bring the ghetto wherever you go!!!

His utterance painfully echoed in my cranium: You don't have to bring the ghetto wherever you go/go/go/go/go/go . . .

I say: Why didn't you just say that from the get-go?

He say: Say what, bro?

I say: Why didn't you just let me know you were a pacifistic racist . . . carrying your badge of liberal privilege in your nose . . . blowin' it whenever you want.

He say: There you go—trying to make this a race thing . . . trying to play the race card.

(And the theater begins to darken . . . the curtain slowly opens . . . and nervously I know there will only be a few more words spoken)

So I hurriedly say: I'm sorry for playing the race card when you're carelessly holding a treasury of overused, marked decks.

(Dramatic race pause . . . highlighted with a stoic Black man gaze.)

I continue: And, by the way, if I'm from the ghetto . . . where are you from?
>Are you from the sitcom suburbs . . .
>Or the transportable trailer parks . . .
>Or the aristocratic white outhouse . . .
>Or from a black-and-white cartoon . . .
>And how did you get in this theater . . .
>And have you ever been to the so-called ghetto
>'Cause there's more creativity/respect
>And love in the ghetto than you'll ever know . . .
>And I'm glad I don't know your name . . .
>And get out of my face . . .
>And . . .

I really didn't get to say all this . . . 'Cause the previews methodically flowed . . . the flick captively rolled . . . Al Pacino satanically glowed . . . And somehow I still enjoyed the show . . . Even though the Devil's Own had cunningly advocated me to an eternal/inescapable hole . . . And all I could do was swallow on an internal moan . . . That echoed in my soul:

GHETTO
GHETTO
GHETTO

'Cause I proudly bring it wherever I go/go/go

Etymology

Circa
1658
Circa
1778
Circa
1888
Around
1998
Master massages own tattered bait
In preparation for copulation with shadow mate
But wait . . . it's late and
Master can't come in queasy slave quarters
Master can't come in trembling urban tenements
To get miscellaneous mistress
Mary Sue or Keisha Blue
Master can't come inside
For it's taboo
To get/to hit
His Black boo
Inside
Slave shack or freedmen's project
Where sickle-celled dreams
Scrape flesh off embryonic soul
But master can come outside
On foot/on knee/on horse
In carriage/in Benz/in unmarked paddy wagon
Can come outside
But master must bring horn (honk/honk)
To beckon

Mary Sue or Keisha Blue
Or Mary's big sis
Mollie, too
Or Keisha's homegirl
Tutu
Or some orphaned girl from another verse
Named
Lulu
'Cause master can perversely flip the 5th-grade slip
And sloppily pump in Lulu
On her 10th birthday
Welcome outside, Lulu
Welcome to presupposed puberty
Compliments of psychopathic master A–Z
Who alphabetically comes wherever the buck he wants
Can come in sugarcane/in cotton field
In hey/in big house/in motel/in alley jail
Can come however he wants
If he just brings horny horn
Honk/honk/honk
And be careful
'Cause soon
Master may interactively come honking for you
To be his virtual 21st-century fugitive anti-soul mate
Horizontally traveling through a perverted
Underground hell road
And the only resistance you may have
Is to stay inside
Muting monotone honks
With polyrhythmic pots and pans
Songs and dance
Tears and cheers
Games and tales

Love and
Next
If your ears still sting
With master's ejaculated vibrations
Just lean out your door
And holler
Stop squeezing that thing, honky
Buzz/buzz . . . fly away, peckerwood
Get out the sun, redneck
Let go of that whip, cracker
'Cause sometimes names are more penetrating
Than phallic swords and seamen bullets
And sometimes names are able to muffle dissonant screeches
Of 2000 seasons of out-of-key horn play

Patience

A lot of Black folk
Will use a
Black doctor/lawyer/dentist
Plumber/gardener/mechanic
Et cetera/et cetera
And have just one bad experience
Just one
And then never use another
Black doctor/lawyer/dentist/
Plumber/gardener/mechanic
Et cetera/et cetera
Again
Never again
But then
Black folk will use
An Arab doctor
A Jewish lawyer
A Japanese dentist
An Irish plumber
A Latino gardener
A Korean mechanic
Or a White/White
Et cetera/et cetera
And have
One/sometimes two/maybe three
Often four/even five
Do I hear six/
More like seven/okay eight
Bad experiences

And still go back
Again and again
And
Again and again
And
Again and again
And Black folk don't do that
Again and again
With each other
'Cause we're programmed with
A self-hating double standard
In which we only give each other
One chance/one try/one attempt/one opportunity
Just one
And only one
And sometimes
Not even one
And I wish we were a little
More patient with each other
At least
Just once

Reparation

Once upon a time
Called always
I asked a partner of mine
If he was registered to vote
He said:
Naw, G
Why the hell should I vote
Votin' don't really change nothin'
Votin' don't really do nothin' for the
Afrocentric/revolutionary/hypo-melanated
BLACKMAN/True God
You know what I'm sayin'

Another partner of mine
Occupyin' the same mind
Space
Replied
In an extended tone:
Well, homie
You know I'm real busy these days
And/well
I just haven't had time
To register
Let alone
Vote
BAM
Was his next decibel
As he threw down a bone

And yelled
"Domino"

Then this righteous sistah
I really respect
Awkwardly said:
Well . . .
You know I'm registered to vote
But damn, brotherman
I haven't really stayed up on the issues
So
I think I'll pass this time
But
Next go around
I'll represent
Well/well
Seems like many of our peeps
Don't wanna vote
Don't know how to vote
And don't know what to vote for
Don't know that young boys and girls
Were gaged with Mississippi urine-drenched ballots
Until their ears and noses bled yellow
So that we could vote
Don't know that grandmothers saturated billy clubs
With blistered and bruised blood
So that we could vote
Don't know that grandfathers had ancestral fingers
Chip/chip CHOPPED off
With crick/crack CRACKERED up
Butcher knifes
But still X'd their names
With crimson blood from severed veins

So that we could vote

Don't know
That if we don't vote
We'll find ourselves livin' in a world
Where Jim Crow is resurrected and elected president
And where Willie Lynch is scientifically reincarnated from a
Time-capsuled decomposed
Putrid test tube
And immediately appointed vice president

Don't know
That if we don't get politically
Active/aware
Beware
We'll find ourselves living in a world where
To be young, gifted, and Black
Is a code phrase
For a COINTELPRO-plan to have ghetto youth
Young, gifted, and addicted to smack
Don't know that if we don't act up
An initiative will pass that makes
Listenin' to rap/havin' braids or locks
And wearin' baggy clothes
All be federal offenses
Punishable by life on
Crack

Don't know that if we don't vote
Historically Black colleges will be eradicated
Affirmative action programs will be annihilated
That the only Blacks at White universities
Will be required to play with the athletic boosters' balls

And that the only place Blacks will receive
Scholarships
Will be at U. Penn/Penn State
Or the penitentiary in any state
'Cause it's one/two/three strikes your out
In the U.S.A.
And
BAM
Will be the sound we'll ubiquitously hear
As our brain cells are eternally slammed
"Domino"

And I don't care how cool we are
If we don't vote
We won't be able to escape the perspiration
Caused by the bureaucratic heat
If we don't grab hold of the ballot
We'll experience infinite millimeter bullets
Shattering our cranial domes
And as we piece back our dismembered collective consciousness
We'll have disunity seizures
Frantically runnin' down the street
Shakin' and breakin'
Realizin'
The Ku Klux Klan has obtained nonprofit status
David Duke is president
Every March 3 is Rodney King Day
Or better yet
National Beat a Nigger Day
And on Thomas Jefferson's birthday it is
Legal for any white male to rape any Black female
As long as he hallucinates through history yellin' Sally
Then we'll all collect accumulated (dis)interest on

Never received reparations
'Cause every Black person will be given 40 acres of
Teenage mutant mule shh

And
Don't go sayin' that votin' don't change nothin'
'Cause
If we don't vote
We'll soon find ourselves pickin'
Spoiled cotton candy with swollen fingers
In jagged cracks through decaying concrete soil
With genocidal pus oozing off split fingertips
'Cause if we don't register
Learn wassup
And check in at the ballot box
We'll soon find ourselves
Propositioned into
Chattel slavery
Talkin' 'bout
Massa
We sho iz wishin' youd set us free
Someday
Someday
Someday

Trippin'

Club lights
flow/float/fly n
flicker
bodies bop
post modern
be
bop
like
rhythmic smiles
sanctioned laughs
no dress code
no cover
from 10 to 12
six-dollar well drinks
reduced
to three
50% keyed
50% freed
men for women
women for men
balanced
equally
reciprocally
playin'
in fun
no deceit
most wack vibes
outside
on 70° street

but inside
everyone just
wants to dance
and will
if asked
nicely/politely
even sadie hawkins
stylé
now
no air-conditioning
but it's still cool
(people and spot)
well
maybe it's
a little hot
but sweat will stop
if you stop groovin'
and roof raisin'
but
you don't stop
and you don't stop
and you don't stop
you know
what
I'm
sayin'
nice stop
and on top
free parking
no valet
but remember
precisely
where

you parked
'cause at 12 o'clock
time stops
as one ill-faded brotha steps
on anotha's
air-protected
little toe
accidentally poppin'
a corn
kernel of pride
and at 12 o'clock
no apology given
and maybe none needed
in crowded spot
pregnant with
strobe-lighted smoke
blinding
and most not minding the
intertwining of
shoes and toes
and most wear bad kicks
anyway
but at 12 o'clock
one brotha
wants/needs/insists
on an
apology
retroactively
at 11:59
or eight/and wait
he even wants a glass
of ice-cubed Hennessy
as recompense

for crunchin'
of little toe
but other brotha gives
no "sorry"
and the only "yack" he gives
is spat and spilled and
laughed at
as he turns
to vanish into
the smoke scattered beat
but other brotha says
"hell no"
and grabs
brothaman's arm
and turns him around
like a lindy
hip hop pirouette
but he don't want to dance
(he want to swing)
he want acknowledgment
of wrong deed
but other brotha
reacts with
redundant body slang
that says
"let go of my ego
let go of my ego
before I put you
in a rusty/crusty
toaster and
pop
you
nigga"

don't know who pulled
or popped
first/or second/or third
but do know
that a head boppin'
backpack floppin'
afro puffin'
young sistah
with no midnight curfew
who got into spot
with fake i.d.
got/got
pulled down
toasted and popped . . .
by two weasels
with type-O syrup
oozing out her chest
and arm
and neck
and leg . . . ooooooooohhhhhhhh
no!
no more head boppin'
no more yes y'allin'
no more roof raisin'
no more fake i.d. n
no more life n
young sista
only one last bitter
cough of sour strawberries
to whip on the salty dance floor
of nigga ego
no more life n
young sista

and
less importantly
but more discussed
(more disgusting)
next week
next month
right now
no more . . . no dress code
no more . . . no cover
no more . . . three-dollar drinks
no more . . . nice spot
so we
off to the
next spot
'cause we don't stop
and we don't stop
and we don't stop
but
we
need
to
stop n
ego
stop ego trippin'
stop n
ego
Stop
&
Grow!

HennaMan

"On your mark . . .
"Get set . . ."
Wait!!!
I'm not in this race
I'm not really Black
Uh Uh
I'm not really Black,
Black
Really . . . Black
This desensitized
Edifice of caramelized Negro
Flesh
Is just a temporary
Full-body
Henna tattoo
You know . . . Henna:
That brownish-red dye
Used to paint skin
And stain hairdos, too
Actually
Last night I snoozed in a crop
Of henna shrubs
Marinating my tropical existence in extra/extra
(Breed all about it . . . in prickly Braille)
Virgin olive oil
Splashing my identity with not-to-right
(Out of a plastic tube)
Lime juice
And scraping off my ancestral weeds with

Jagged cowrie shells
But now I'm Henna and Proud
Down for the Henna Struggle
100% Henna
Henna centric
Revolutionary HennaMan
And you don't know what the HennaMan goes through
And
Did I tell you
I'm not really Black . . .
That this is a brother tattoo
And
Can someone get me a glass of Hennessy
Please
'Cause in six to eight daze
My henna consciousness will fade
And I'll be half a henna
A henna mulatto
A half henna breed
A mixed henna
And
Another glass of Henny please
'Cause in a week and one fourth
My brittle being will recede
And I'll be a henna quadroon
Eight hours later
I'll wither into
A henna octoroon
I'll be transfixed in an hourly-changing
Racial monsoon
And they'll call me RA
And not R-A-W
Or RA like omnipotent

Egyptian Sun God
Or Ra like rapper Rakim
Naw
I'll just be racially androgynous
RA
Too henna for some
But not henna enough for others
And finally
In two sleek identity weeks
I'll be back to abnormal
For I'll just be
Dangling slabs of ambiguous skin
Carelessly hanging on to rickety political bone
Awkwardly searching for the finish line
Of my
Race . . .
"Go!!!"

Part 2

◎

Blues, Blushes,
Brushes, and
Bruises of Blunted
Love

Ph.D.

I thirst for your enticing scholarly double-mint whispers
That whiz me through your curious curriculum
Allowing me to penetrate your
Body
Of enlightened/uplifted spiritual bliss
(Oh yeah . . . I hunger for your enigmatic, edifying, edible education of
erotica)
I crave to be your star pupil
Fixated on your
Pupils
Lashes
Brows
And even breezing around the placid plateaus of your indigenous
Cheekbones
But no group training, please
Only private sessions . . .
Mano y mano
Torso on torso
Third eyelid through third eyelid
Where
I seek to study your moon-ripened/shadow-laced
Attention-filled/generally required
Nipples
While intermittingly interpreting
The structural dynamics of your postmodern/curvilinear
Hips
(Aah!)
I yearn to explore the existential reality
Of your underanalyzed

Feet
Focusing on the alchemy of
My saliva
Interspersed between your slightly ticklish
Toes
'Cause I want to get high
Higher learning
And philosophize about the paradox of the prodigious
Future that firmly rests behind you
Butt
Somehow loosely jiggles in front of me
I want my oral exams beginning on your paradigm-shifting
Suction-cupped/organically slide-projected
Lips
Butt ending on your wet dream–provoking/ever-elusive
Hyposensitive/reclusive upper-inner thighs
And though I often forget
I'll remember to gently dot all your eyes
And playfully cross all your Ti/T's
As I copiously take notes
On your Freudian-flattened/vegetarian-smoothened
Stomach
With invisible ink flowing from the crevices of my felt-tip
Tongue
(No time for a study break)
'Cause in the nearsighted future
I'll have my dissertation
Challenged and defended by every complex counterposition your
Physique
Can safely contrive
As I repetitiously explore the tender contours of your tenured
Womb
(Looks like it's going to be an all-nighter)

And do you have any royal jelly?/ginseng?/yohimbe?
So I can have another hour to devour
Your required feeling
Until I have my graduate education
Validated by your earth moans
Hooded by your rhythmic gyrations
And endorsed with your fingernail signature
'Cause ultimately
I want my Ph.D. conferred
Well inside of you
Only then
Can you call me a doctor . . .
Doctor

Wet Massage

The first time you gave me a massage
I tingled all over
Ooh
Easy on that spot baby
I'm kinda sore there
And when your touch got a little wet
Drifting around my shining spine . . .
I decided
I ain't going to work tomorrow
Ooh
And the tip of your stroke felt like an itsy-bitsy ballerina
Pirouetting from side to tingly side
Ha/ha/haaah . . . I'm ticklish there
Then your dripping tool of caress began steaming
And so it did a little slip-n-slide from my neck bone
Down my slippery torso, and pausing at my (Ooooh)
But that ride didn't chill your searing glands
'Cause it started gettin' even hotter and hotter . . .
And you're scorching me, baby
So your mouth's overseer whipped back
And I thought to myself
Damn . . . the chills, and the tingles, and the Oohs are all gone,
But ecstasy's scepter resurfaced
After a refueling with saliva
Then slithered to my lower back
Climbed to my neckbone
And leaped off my shoulder
And I turned to make sure you wouldn't
Hit the stucco sky

But

Your taste buds fell in my hearing

Ooh!!!!!!!!!!!!!!!!!!!!!!!!!!!!!!!!!!!!!!Ha

And my body started gyrating and I looked like I was trying to bring
    back break dancin'

And I said "no mo . . . no mo"

But you heard "slow mo . . . slow mo"

As you pop-locked my audibles

Moistenin' my lobes as you gently jumped away

With your hand mimicking below

And then you cocked back your head and asked

"Is everything alright, baby?"

But before I could answer you swallowed my voice . . .

And I said "Ooh, Ooh, Ooh . . ."

And you repeated "is everything alright, baby?"

And I moaned "Ahh . . . now it is"

Completion

I got so
Much love to give you
And
Not so much love
But
Soul much love
The kind of love that comes
From
Way
Deep
Down
Inside
My
Soul
Filled with all my
Passions
Dreams
Fears
Pains
Joys
And
Really
My soul
Is all that's left
For me to give
'Cause I've already given you
My heart
My body
And

My mind
And
Now
All that's left
For me to give you
Is my soul
Full of love

Jealousy

I went flying beyond the sky last night
Floating in darkness
While the moon and stars dreamed in another space
Scared
Cold
Alone in the universe
I waited for eternity to slip away
But silence kept me awake
Waiting
Waiting
And while waiting
A thought of you flickered
Suddenly
Super-stars appeared
Showing off
Shining
Radiating
Glowing
Exploding
And I smiled to myself
Knowing the universe
Was
Jealous
Of the glittering thought
I just had of you

Annoy Me*

This morning the bed felt very small
No pillow
No sheets
You had it all
If not for the wall
I'd have woke up on the floor

You annoy me . . . so what

When I unpeel my eyes
From this abandoned state
I see your bare feet march to the bathroom door
I hear you start to brush your teeth
Which means I must wait five minutes or more

You annoy me . . . so what

When I take my turn in the restless room
The seat is down
The toothpaste deformed
The mirrors fogged
The water cold
And one sheet left on the roll

You annoy me . . . so what

*Originally written as a song with Jason Luckett.

I stumble to the kitchen
You are at the table
Lost in the *Times*
I mix your pancake batter
I make your morning brew
I flip the cakes
I squeeze the juice
I scramble the eggs
Can you give me a break

You annoy me . . . so what
You annoy me . . . so what
You annoy me . . .
So what . . .
We've got the rest of the day.

Against Common Sense

"Damn"
That's what I said
When I first saw you
"Damn"
That's what I say
When I still see you
"Damn"
Lord have mercy
And I ain't usin' the Lord's name
In vain
'Cause the Lord made me a believer
In the power of miracles
When he created the fineness of you
And in bed with you
Hmm/hmm/hmm
I'm born again
Hallelujah
But
There's just one little problem
That I thought I could get around
Overlook/ignore
And
This is kinda hard for me to say
But
You see
I ah
Umm
Well
It's like this

Where you were blessed with
External/aesthetic/physical
Beauty
You were retarded with commonsensical
Knowledge
And
Maybe you weren't born like this
Maybe you've just always been so fine
That you haven't had to think
That you've been able to let your intellect exist on
Cruise control
But whether genetically or sociologically explained
The result is the same
Your brain cells are out of shape/overweight
And let's not confuse overweight with heavy
'Cause when I try to pry into your deepest thoughts
I end up floatin' just above a mountaintop
And when you really try to get deep
I end up havin' to give you
Mouth-to-mouth
Just to shut you up before
You suffocate me with confusion
I mean
Talkin' to you is like talkin' on a
Cellular phone whose battery is on low—
Sometimes you're there
Rational/even clear
But inevitably
Your conversation just dies
(Hello)
And I've tried
But I haven't found the device
That recharges you

And
No
I don't wanna go to a movie with you today . . .
No
I don't wanna go to dinner with you tonight
But
We can we go to a library
And get you a card
And get you checked out or checked in
Or
How 'bout some nice jazz
Let's get a *LA Weekly*
And see who's in town
And look
Kenny Garrett
Miles Davis' ex-sax man is around
Jammin' with some other young jazz titans
Like Roy Hargrove
Charnett Moffett
Jeff "Tain" Watts
And
You've heard of Kenny
What
He's your favorite jazz musician
Really
You even have some of his albums
Which ones
Songbird
Breathless
Wait a millennium
Not Kenny G
Kenny Garrett
You see what I mean

And I've tried
To show you the light
And I've put patience in front of me
But it's rapidly fading away
As the sun of your internal beauty
Is eclipsed
And perhaps our relationship
Should slip away too
But
There's just one little problem
That I thought I could get around
Overlook/ignore
Well
You see
This is the twentieth time
I've written this poem
'Cause
Damn/damn/damn
You sure is fine
And
Let's not go out this morning
'Cause I wanna be born again
And again
And again
And
Lord have mercy
Look at me
Talkin' 'bout you ain't got no common sense
When I'm the one selling my soul
Just to be born again

Goodwill

So
I'm goin' through my bedroom drawers
Throwin' out everything I ain't used
In the last three seasons
But I'm not really convertin' unused clothes
Into wasted cotton trash
Instead
I'm pick/pick/packin' 'em
And plantin' 'em in a
Playhouse-large big-screen TV box
And
Admittedly the task is tediously
Overwhelming
And excitement-wise
Underwhelming
Until I come to my third drawer
Where
Mixed in between pairless socks
And too shrunk/underarm-stained T-shirts
I found you
And not a deliberately misplaced picture of you
Not a clumsily hidden voodoo doll of you
Not a nostalgic mothball thought of you
Not anything
But you
And I held you up to see if you still fit
I dropped you on my bed to see if you still had some fluff
And I even tried you on to see if you were still in style
But the answer was NO/NO/NO

To all of the above
So I thought about usin' you as a
Makeshift household duster
But I didn't want to upset my delicate furniture
With your abrasiveness
So I thought about sky hookin' you into
My gettin' ready to be emptied wastebin
But I didn't want to offend the garbage with your company
So
I just folded you up
Until you folded no more
And tossed you into the box with the
Other unwanted rags
So that somebody else might get
Some use out of you

Afro Bluesiatic Blues

I.

Your saliva-marinated fingerprints
Slithered against my
Sweat-glistened
Overheated
Insatiated flesh
Penetrating the fragile
Walls of my bedridden
Sensuality
And
I
Want to strategically
Strike back
At your AfroBlueBlackBack
But
My fingernail arsenal
Is depleted from an earlier
Nervous war
But
Inspired by the Trane
I cunningly use to transport you . . .
I improvise
Dah dah dah dah dah . . . dah dah dah
Dah dah dah dah dah . . . Afro-Blue
And
I take the ten(inch)or
A little less sax
That you skillfully blew earlier

And I swing
And I blow
And I bob
And I climb
And I reach
And I'm almost out of breath
But you dig it
So I keep diggin'
And
Dah dah dah dah dah . . . dah dah dah
Dah dah dah dah dah . . . dah (ugh) dah (ugh)
UGH!

II.

But
What am I doin' in this sacred bed
With you
Except
Profanely sexing?

III.

Of course
I savor our cataclysmic passion
Highlighted with pelvic bones smashin'
Always vergin' on nuclear orgasm
But I don't really appreciate you as much
As I do doin' the do—
                    Dah dah dah

IV.

What an orgasmic revelation!
What a glaucomic eradication!
What vision!
What clarity!
"I see"
Said the closed-eyed man.

V.

And
Oh
After the nut has gone
How could I lead you on
When love was never around
Oh . . . ooohhh . . . oooooohhhhhh
After the nut has gone
What was never right is still wrong
'Cause love with you I ain't found.

VI.

(Saxophone solo.)

VII.

Where is the poetry
In being a player?
Where is the bliss

In being a mack?
How can I be spiritually lush
When I'm just trying to crush a lot?

VIII.

I need more evaluation
And less ejaculation . . .
I need a new game inserted
In my autobiographical play station!

IX.

But if I quit
Will I know how to love?
Will I know how to flush out flesh from love?
Will I be too analytical/intellectual to love?
Will I be able/capable of maintaining
Nonbiodegradable love?

X.

Thirty's rite around the corner
Of my sanity
Three/two/one
(Buzzzzzzzzzzzzz)
Dah dah dah dah dah . . . dah dah dah dah
Dah dah dah dah dah . . . dah
                    da
                         DAH!

The Truth

Just hanging
On to venetian-blinded
Sather-gated
Sat. day
Check-mated sunset
In lost best
Final Four/spring break in
Not awakened
UC Berkeley
Need key to get in
Barrows Hall
Window gawking
At glowing Goddess
Left/Right iris stalking
Light speed
Tongue talking
Nature balking
Hold on
Stay strong
My molten
(Where you going?)
Soul sister
You got another long
Campanile chime-rotation
Tintinnabulation
To sear
Over here
Through my window
Sill and p.c. screen
And please/please

Don't leave . . .
You're my right now
I'm writing (wow!) inspiration
My microspore nap sac for word pollination
My healing potion for ill incantations
You great big ball of
Bounce/Bounce
Feel the okay
Cliché fire
But
Look at mischievous me
Mired in what can't be
Like wishing for maple tree leaves
To cease waving in March breeze
Please
Overly scholastic/impatiently bombastic
Lascivious me
Savoring my life/my life/my life
In the pun-shine
Not yet rhymed
Sublimed
With phantasmagoric
Alas
Allegoric
Knighted constellations
Celestial sensations
Ah
What creation
The finger
To pen
To (my or your) pad
To hug
To coo
To spoon

To soothe
To bed
Wet transmagical trick or treats
Of the twi-hi-night-light
But it's all right
'Cause I've just
Discovered/recovered
Uncharted stars
Glimmering
Telescopically glistening in your
Bambi-fawning eyes
Flickering
Fulfilling the yawning space
In between my ego's bickering
(Woman, are you listening?)
You got me shimmering
Shh/shh
Shivering with Big Bang erection/Black Hole connection
Parallel universe intersection
Traversed with my solar system mate
Elliptically straight
(I feel grrrreat)
Fated with
Mercury passion
Venus secretion
Earth salvation
Mars sensation
Jupiter laughter
Saturn burns
Uranus chaos
Neptune croons
Plato orgasm
Tabbatha "Milky Way" Mays
Guess what?

In
   your
      galaxy
        I
          have
            come
              to
                stay

Part 3

Cornucopia of Culturally Colored Commentary

All That and a Bag of Words

Have you ever noticed that Black folk have a way of takin'
Words that mean one thang
And turnin' 'em 'round so that they mean anotha
Like when a brotha's talkin' 'bout a beautiful sistah
An' he says this sistah is phat
But not fat like overweight or obese
'Cuz this sistah's fresh
An' not fresh like she's got attitude
Or fresh like she's inexperienced
'Cuz this girl's tight
But not tight like uptight or stiff
'Cuz this girl's dope
And not dope like the stuff some of us smoke
'Cuz this girl's fine
But not fine like "just awright" or fine like "that'll do"
'Cuz this woman's proper
And not proper like formal or genteel
'Cuz this woman's a freak
But not like some Freddy Krueger–type freak
'Cuz this honey's the shh
And not like the stinky shh
'Cuz this honey's fly
But not like the buzz, buzz flyin' fly that hangs around the hummin' shh
'Cuz this sistah's the bomb
And not a bomb
But the bomb
'Cuz this sistah's all of that
But not all of that like all of the above
'Cuz this sistah's above all that
That's above all

And that's not all
'Cuz she's live, and she's got flavor, and she's top-notch, and she's hype
And this sistah's just all of that and a bag of words
But not just any ol' bag of words
But a bag of our words, with our meanings
That's what she is
She's all that and a bag of our words
With our meanings
That's all!

Jazz Is Is

So when did Kenny G become a jazz great
'Cause I never knew he was a jazz musician in the first place
Now don't get me wrong
I don't mean to disrespect Kenny
Or any of his devoted fans
'Cause I understand that different folks got
Different musical tastes
And that's cool
But I also understand that jazz is a unique musical expression
That should not be mocked or mimicked by loose definitions or massive
    misunderstandings
Now jazz is many things
Like jazz is straight-ahead
Like Bird, Dizzy, Mingus, and Monk
Jazz is soft, warm, romantic, sensual, and passionate
Like playin' some Dexter Gordon while makin' love—Right 'round
    midnight
Jazz is spiritual, existential, metaphysical, and quite essential
Like John Coltrane—
A Love Supreme . . . A Love Supreme . . . A Love Supreme . . .
Need I say more
Jazz is vocal and jazz is lyrical
Like Ella, Sarah, Dinah, and Billie
So melodious, so harmonious, so rich, so true
Jazz is BIG—like Duke's big band takin' the A Train, B Train, C Train,
    and not stoppin' till they've
Created their own Z Train
Jazz is small—like Pharaoh Sanders and Sonny Rollins blowin' a secret
    in your ear
(Hush hush)

Jazz is even strange, bizarre, "out there"
Like some of them wild, mystical, cosmic places Ornette Coleman and
    Sun Ra like to go
And jazz changes—again and again and over again
Miles showed us this
From *Bebop* to *Kind of Blue* to *Bitches Brew* to *Time After Time*
Again and again and over again
Yeah, jazz is change and change is jazz.
But no matter how much jazz changes . . . jazz is jazz . . . no matter
    what
Jazz fills in all kinds of space
Jazz improvises and innovates
Jazz feels, moves, touches, and soothes
Jazz floats and digs and climbs and screams
Jazz is is as is is jazz—jazz is
Jazz is all of that and all of that is jazz
And if jazz ain't all of that
It just ain't jazz
And if jazz ain't jazz
It ain't fusion jazz
'Cause that implies jazz is somehow fusin' with something else
But that ain't happenin'
'Cause jazz is like Black folks
If jazz mixes with anything else that anything else is jazz
It's the one drop of jazz rule
And it don't sound like Kenny G
Or any of the stuff they play on the wave is mixed with jazz at all
So it ain't even fusion jazz
It's more like Confusion or Con-fusion
And that ain't jazz
'Cause jazz is not is not jazz
Jazz is is as is is jazz—jazz is
Jazz is all of that and all of that is jazz
That's jazz and jazz is just that
And that ain't Kenny G!

It's a Big Joke

The other night I was watching some
Late-night Black comedy show
And I sat there watchin' comedian
After comedian/after comedian
For about thirty minutes
And in that thirty minutes
I don't think I heard one joke
Not one
Not even half a one
All I heard was a buncha nonsense that
Made my ears wanna go def
And that put my brain in a serious jam
'Cause all I heard was nigga after nigga
After some more nigga
Nigga mixed with profanity
Profanity topped with vulgarity
Vulgarity laced with obscenity
Obscenity pregnant with egoism
Egoism giving birth to sexism
Sexism transformed into misogyny
Misogyny coupled with homophobia
Homophobia reinforced by xenophobia
Xenophobia synthesized with stupidity
Stupidity demonstrated by immaturity
Immaturity made venomous by ignorance
And ignorance catapulted into
A complicated realm of buffoonery . . .
Creating a frustrating situation
In which
After watching thirty minutes of modern-day

Black comedy
I realized that it wasn't funny
Now don't get me wrong
I don't want to sound like some
Neoconservative/anti–first amendment/put some soap in their mouths/
ban them from the universe/throw 'em in an institution/Rush Limbaugh/
Pat Robertson/Clarence Thomas type
I'm just a cat who wants to hear some real comedy
With some real jokes
By some real comedians
With some real dignity
Really
Now
This doesn't mean that I think Black comedians
Should stop swearing
Shoot
I've even used a
MF
In a poem or two
And
Heck
Richard Pryor is my favorite laugh-making man
And
That Negro
Use to
Cuss his butt off
But Richard had routines with
Real insights
Really
Like when he said:
"Cops don't shoot cars . . . they shoot nig-gars"
Real funny
But deep
Too

But today a lot of Black comedians are about as deep
As their own untied shoelaces
Dangerously dragging
Just above a dirty ground
Which is to say
Today
A lot of Black comedians are lazily
Being nasty for nasty sake
And damn
My ears are going def
And my brain is a jam
'Cause I can't understand why
We continue to support this nonsense
And why we continue to tune in to watch this buffoonery
And why we continue to spend money to view this stupidity
And why we continue to allow our comedians
To do comedy in which there is no humor
None
Not even half of
None
But then again
There is one big joke of blind and def acceptance
One big joke of jammed confusion
One big joke that punchlines us
And
The jokes on us, y'all
Yeah . . .
The jokes on us
Ha/Ha/Ha/Ha
Very funny
MF

Gluteus Maximus Addictus Poem

A lot of men
Need to go to AA
And not AA as in
Alcoholics Anonymous
But AA as in
Assoholics Anonymous
'Cause a lot of men are straight
Addicted to ass
These are the men that
No matter what
Can't see past a women's butt
These are the men that will
Hurt their loved ones—for ass
Lose their jobs—for ass
Go broke—for ass
Drop out of school—for ass
Dis their friends—for ass
And even wreck their cars
While lookin' at ass
(Damn "ass-drunk" drivers)
These are the men that are so
Addicted to ass
They'll always make
Butt statements
Like
The women's personality is wack
BUTT
She's got much backs

Or
The women's breath is kinda hummin'
BUTT
She's gotta a plump ol' onion
(Ta-dow)
BUTT/BUTT/BUTT
These men are all about
Butt
So much so that they forget about such things as
Personality/compatibility/and spirituality
'Cause they're assoholics
Only lookin' for ass
And more ass
And much more ass
And
Like I said
They need to take their butts to
Assoholics Anonymous
And cure their dumb asses
But?

To Be or Not to Be

To be or not to be
To be or not to be
A mack
Now there is a question for the ages
To be or not to be
A mack

To be a mack
To live carelessly, vicariously, and loosely
To meet lots n lots of women
And try n hit each and everyone
To be smooth, suave, slick, and sly
To have a nice rap
To have fresh lines
To get the most numbers
To meet and hit in the same night
To hit more than one or more than two
Again in one night
To hit two or three at the same time
Still in one night
To be a mack daddy
Pimp Daddy
And to have women call you daddy
To be a player
To play around
To play games
To play with minds
To play with hearts
To play for play sake
To be involved with one

And mess around with another
And another
And another's other
To mack, to run mack, to throw mack, to be mackin', to be a Big Mac
To mickadeemickadeemickadeemickadee mack
To lie, to cheat, to hurt, to deceive, to betray, to confuse, to manipulate
To bow wow wow yeepe yo yeepe yé—DOG
To be a mack
Hmm

Not to be a mack
Not to be slick
Not to be sly
Not to use tired ol' lines
Not to be corny, cornier, or corniest
Not to creep or be a creep
Not to sneak or sneak peak
Not to be a creepy, sneaky, peaky freak
Not to always try to do the freaky deaky (or what)
Not to think of women as bitches, hoes, skeezers, tenders, tenderonis,
    honeys, honey dips, tricks, biscuits, or as
Whatevers
Not to mack, run mack, throw mack, be mackin', or be a Big Mac
Not to mickadeemickadeemickadeemickadee mack
Not to be a mack
To be gentle
To be a man
To be a gentle man
To be faithful, honest, sincere, and up-front
To be kind, giving, sharing, and warm
(Not to be cold)
To be a player
But to play with only one
Your one and only one

To play games of love, romance, sensuality, passion, and ecstasy
With one special someone
Not two special someones
Or several special someones
But one special someone
Your one and only one
Not to be a mack
Hmm

So there it is
To be or not to be
To hoe or not to hoe
To pimp or not to pimp
To play or not to play
To mickadeemickadeemickadeemickadee mack
Or not to mickadeemickadeemickadeemickadee mack
To bow wow wow yeepe yo yeepe yé
Or not to bow wow wow yeepe yo yeepe yé
There it is
A question for the ages
To be or not to be
A mack
And brothas
You know the right answer
Or do you
To be continued

Doesn't Make You a Man

Doesn't make you a man
To go around town
Playin' around
Tryin' to get a woman's
Pants down
Doesn't make you a man

Doesn't make you a man
To be
A mack/a player/a pimp/a gigolo
Or any other euphemistic ho
No
Doesn't make you a man

Doesn't make you a man
To simply say
"I'm a man"
Or "I'm the man"
'Cause simply sayin'
You're a man
Or the man

Doesn't really make you a man
No/man
I'm not playin'
When I'm sayin'
That just sayin'
You're a man
Doesn't make you a man

Doesn't make you a man
To call another man
A freak/a queer/a sissy/a faggot
Or some other "non-manly" word
Particularly when you're at home
Masturbating over pictures of
Women kissin'/an' lickin'/an' rubbin'/an' touchin'
Other women
You hypocritical/double-standardized
Contradictory/homophobic maggot
Don't you know that
What you're sayin'
Doesn't make you a man

Doesn't make you a man
To think that
Because you're a man
That no means yes
No
All parts understood
No
No/no
Hey/hey
Hoe/hoe
Patriarchy has got to go
And if you don't think so
Doesn't make you a man

Doesn't make you a man
To throw out your hand
To slap/to push/to beat/to hurt
A woman
In any kind of way
No way

Okay . . . O. J.
O. J. it's not okay
To slap/an push/an beat/an hurt
A woman
In any kind of way
Guilty or innocent
It's not okay
And it
Doesn't make you a man

What makes you a man
Is breaking from all the
Stereotypical receptions of
Being a man
It's being the opposite
The inverse
The other side of what you think
Being a man is
It's being honest
Not just to others
But to yourself
It's being kind/considerate/compassionate
Open/revealing/vulnerable
And willing to liberate tears
It's being tuned into
The feminine
As well as
Masculine side of you
And
If you don't understand
Well
Man
All I got to say
Is all that I've been saying

Which is to say
All the things you're doing
That you think
Make you a man
Really
Doesn't make you a man
No/man
You know what I'm saying

Road Rage

We don't need any
more Land Cruisers. Beep! Instead
We need some land. Honk!!!

Why I Would Never Buy a Jeep Cherokee

This country
America
The so-called beautiful
Ignores the religious freedom of
The native people
Steals water and other natural resources from
The native people
Dumps toxic waste onto the lands of
The native people
Pumps gin and whiskey juice into the homes of
The native people
And
Fails to live up to over 400 treaties signed with
The native people
But then
This country
America
The so-called beautiful
Proclaims to honor
The native people
By naming sports teams
After them
Teams like
The Atlanta Braves
The Cleveland Indians
The Chicago Black Hawks
The Washington Redskins
The Kansas City Chiefs

The Florida State Seminoles
And
The University of Illinois Fighting Illini
But
That's not honoring
That's objectifying
That's caricaturizing
That's humiliating
That's stereotyping
That's degrading
That's exploiting
And
That's the same as
Having teams like
The San Francisco Sambos
The Jackson State Jungle Bunnies
The Seattle Spearchuckers
The New Orleans Niggers
The Detroit Darkies
The Cincinnati Coons
The San Diego Spics
The Green Bay Greasers
The Baltimore Beaners
The Washington Wetbacks
The Chicago Chinks
The Golden State Gooks
The Kansas City Kikes
The St. Louis Semites
The New Jersey Jews
The New York Hymies
The Houston Honkies
The Oklahoma Ofays
The UCLA Crackers
The Phoenix Rednecks

The Pittsburgh Peckerwoods
The Wichita White Trash
And
The Brigham Young Blue-eyed Devils
But
That's not honoring
That's objectifying
That's caricaturizing
That's humiliating
That's stereotyping
That's degrading
That's exploiting
And
That's why I would never buy a Jeep Cherokee
Never buy a Jeep Cherokee
Jeep Cherokee never buy
Never buy
Never . . .
Buy
Never . . .
Bye

Higher Learning

What is high
What is higher
What is learn
What is learnin'
What is higher learnin'
What it is
I mean
What is it
What is higher learnin'

Well
I went and got me some
Higher learnin'
And found out
What higher learnin'
Is . . .
It's learnin' 'bout Europe
Learnin' 'bout White folks
Learnin' 'bout the West
And not learnin' 'bout the rest
It's learnin' that folks of color ain't got no
Teachings to learn from
That's higher learnin'
That's what it is

What is higher learnin'
What it is
It's learnin' that if not for slavery
Black folks would be runnin' 'round
Butt-naked in Africa . . .

Spear-chuckin' and jungle-runnin'
It's learnin' that Christopher Columbus
Disc-covered America
And terrorized. . . . I mean
Civilized the so-called Indians
It's learnin' that Egypt was white
That Jesus was white
That Moses was white
That Pharaoh was white
That Hannibal was white
That Cleopatra was white
And that anybody else that
Did anything else
Was also white
That's higher learnin'
That's what it be

What is higher learnin'
It's learnin' in
A bastion
For Eurocentric indoctrination
It's learnin' in an environment that is mostly white
Complete with white professors
White TAs
White chancellors
White administrators
White authors of
White books
White university police
White alumni
White sponsorship
And mostly white students
That's higher learnin'

That's what it is
That's what it be

What is higher learnin'
It's another way of sayin'
Higher deception
Higher trickery
Higher indoctrination
Higher manipulation
Higher brainwashing
Higher miseducation . . .
But to keep us confused
They just call it
Higher Learnin'
That's higher learnin'
That's what it is
That's what it be
That's it
Or is it
(WHAT)

Too Many

Back in the day
I don't remember going to
Or hearing about
Too many funerals
Except for when grandmas and grandpas
Died of old age
But
In this day
I see and hear about
Too many funerals
All the time
Funerals for victims of drive-bys
Funerals for victims of gang warfare
Funerals for victims of police brutality
And why are there so many funerals in this day
Funerals for victims of carjackings
Funerals for victims of drunk driving
Funerals for victims of reckless driving
And where are the funerals for folks
Dying of old age
'Cause all I see are
Funerals for victims of crack
Funerals for victims of nicotine
Funerals for victims of alcohol abuse
Funerals for victims of hyperstress
Funerals for victims of heart attacks
Funerals for victims of kidney collapse
And where are the funerals for folks
Dying of old age
'Cause all I see are

Funerals for victims of rape
Funerals for victims of spousal abuse
Funerals for victims of penis-driven patriarchy
And where are the funerals for folks
Dying of old age
Where are they
'Cause all I see are
Funerals for victims of AIDS
And
Funerals for victims of AIDS
And
Funerals for victims of AIDS
And
Does anybody have a cure for AIDS
'Cause I don't wanna go to any more
Funerals for victims of AIDS
And where are the funerals for folks
Dying of old age
'Cause all I see are
Funerals for victims of starvation
Funerals for victims of homelessness
Funerals for victims of hopelessness
Funerals for victims of suicide
And why are there so many funerals in this day
Funerals for victims of
White on Black
Black on Black
Black on Brown
Brown on Yellow
Yellow on Tan
White on Red
Red on Red
White on White
And

Everybody else on everybody else
Violence
Too many
Funerals for victims of
Everybody on Everybody violence
And where are the funerals for folks
Dying of old age
'Cause all I see are funerals for folks
Dying from going to
Too many funerals
Too many
Too many
Funerals
Too many
Too many
Dying
And
Does anybody
Die of old age anymore
Anybody
Die
Die
Dead

Part 4

Rainbow
Transfusions

The Fire in the Drum

(For Matt Crawford: 1903–1996)

How do we embrace a blazing revolutionary spirit
How do we hug and massage a bay burning legacy
How do we booby trap a courageous fire
And suspend its essence on root-strong fingertips
And flick calcium-enriched flames to burn free
The manifold hapless frozen souls
Who carelessly make the world a silly/chilly
Frosty the snowflake place
How do we resist the deceptively warm temptations of complacency
And butterfly stroke our way upstream
In subzero/subhuman oil-burdened waters
Even when our thighs/forearms/and bottom lips
Are memory-shackled and identity-gaged
With 400-year-strong
Transatlantic seaweed
How do we ice pick through the pain
How do we chisel through the chills
How do we defrost the frozen lives
How do we resist/rebel/and Re-Heal
Let us begin by calling out the names of those
Who gracefully held their breath in smoke-burdened crevices
So that future generations could effortlessly breathe
We mouth-to-mouth names like
Sojourner/and Denmark/and Gabriel/and Harriet/and Walker
And Dunbar/and McCoy/and Nat
We ignite flames with high-octane names like
Fannie Lou/and Mary Church/and Carter G/and Ida B/and A. Phillip
And Ossie D/and Ruby Dee/and Marcus G/and Jimmy B/and W.E.B.

We conjure wildfires/wildflowers/and wildlife with names like
Louise/and Rosa/and Patterson/and Bethune/and Drew/
And Medgar/and Ella/and Angela/and Mahalia/and Martin/
And Marvin/and Aretha/and Ali/and X
We invite the sun's passion to sizzle flesh by shouting names like
Trane/and Sonia/and Gwendolyn/and Dizzy/and Micheaux/and
    Roach/and Dunham/and
Catlett/and Barnes/and Lawrence/and Bearden/and Morrison/and
    Ringgold/and Mfume
And Maxine/and Dellums
And if these names don't snap/pop/and crackle with familiarity
We parachute into the belly of volcanoes
And formally introduce ourselves to molten spirits
And write their names with lava across our chests
And then
With sudden heart burns
Incurred from overloading on spiritual soul fool
We roar out a quilt of acid names
And
Shhhhhhhhhhhhhhhhhhhh
Listen
'Cause at this moment
(Which is all moments)
We hear a single name (Matt)
A sweat lodge name that causes our maladies to perspire away
A tiger balm name that strengthens bones in the sauna of tradition
Matt Crawford
Doing Business As
A
Life lover/change maker/freedom dancer/dream enhancer/humble
    leader
Oppression hater/heart traveler/soul(full) radical/truth-giver/knowledge
    spreader

Root chiropractor/Juju spirit/Maasai warrior
Pain taker/love creator/fire maker
Son/father/husband/grandfather
Friend
To me
And you/and you
And we sever vocal cords by yelling his name (Matt)
We tie-dye ku klux klan sheets with his righteousness (Matt)
We turn marijuana into sage
Cocaine into talcum powder
Crack into cowrie shells
And 40 ounces of malt liquor into wheat grass and aloe vera juice
With his scream for change (Matt)
We convert crips and bloods into new millennia griots and healers with
    his memory (Matt)
We transform Republicans/Democrats/Independents/and unregistereds
Into communialists with his vocalized vision (Matt)
We make humans . . . wordly humanitarians with his smile and his laugh
    (Matt)
And we make the 21st century a new universe(al) order with his heated
    heart (Matt)
And when we are through making magic in the furnace of change
We hear his voice reverberate in our veins
And we feel our souls warm-up
And we see him grin as we
FINALLY
Embrace the love tradition/the human mission
THE FIRE VISION
And our hearts become
Jimbes/and bongos/and congas/and darabukas/and tsuzumis
And timpanis/and naqqaras/and tom-toms/and tambourines/and 808s
And we hear Matt restfully beat the words
Well done

Well done
Well done
And we
Become the fire in the drum

Prelude to a Memory

With a fragile edition of Einstein's
Theory of Relativity
Infinitely dangling from his grasp
The Wednesday night poet
Awakens from a triply bypassed art attack
With a snake from yesterday
Weaving through his throat today
Tickling his tongue tomorrow
Reminding the naive image connoisseur
That his past is super-glued
To his present
And suction-cupped to his future
Somewhere in the 5th dimension of the present
Genuflection toward the galaxy
Has taught this alien under the sun
That the Present/Past/Future
Coexist in a velvet
Black hole
Demystifying linear conceptions of
Crystal time
Pulling memory through
Eternal astral animation
Informing the wordanaut
That he has no choice
But to always
Remember . . .

Remember

Remember when a wall of rainbow beads took you from one room
Into another
And remember when carpet was all shag and all shaggy
Even in the bathroom
And remember those velvet pictures that seemed to be in
Every Black livin' room
Like the one with a beautiful, strong Black man
And a beautiful, strong Black woman
Both displayin' beautifully picked Afros
And both displayin' beautiful dark brown skin
And both just displayin' beauty and blackness—together
On velvet
Remember . . .
And remember on the other side of the livin' room
Diagonal to the strobe light and right above the beanbag
There was a picture of another strong Black man
With a well-defined arm reachin' down a wall to help another
Black man
'Cause he ain't heavy . . . he's my brother
Remember . . .
Remember when there weren't any bars on windows
And when drive-bys were a thing of the future
And when the word crip was used to describe disabled people
And when the word blood was used to acknowledge everybody
Like . . . what's happenin' blood
Remember . . .
Remember when even white folks were trying to have Afros
And when Jheri curls had not yet been invented
But when brothas had perms that looked better than the sistahs'
Remember . . .

Remember when Michael Jordan was Dr. J and Emmitt Smith was O. J.
  Simpson and Barry Bonds was Reggie Jackson and Evander Holyfield
  was Muhammad Ali—The Greatest
The Greatest of all time
And the Greatest Love of All
Remember . . .
Remember pukka shells, and mood rings, and 8-track tapes, and
  whitewall tires, and bell-bottom pants, and butterfly-collar shirts, and
  platform shoes with goldfish in them
And remember big caddies, and big pimps, and little phrases like
Groovy, Right On, Hey Baby, and Dig It
Yeah, dig it y'all . . . diamond in the back, sunroof top
Diggin' the scene with a gangsta lean . . . oooooh
Remember . . .
Remember dashikis, and Afros and Afro picks with Black power fists
Just to remind us that power could come with a simple flick of
The wrist
And remember watchin' flicks like *Superfly, Dolomite, Cooley High,*
  Cleopatra Jones, Blackula, Black Caesar, Three the Hard Way,
  The Mack
And that cat who was a bad mother—(SHUT YOUR MOUTH)
Just talkin' 'bout Shaft
And remember the music
And not just the listenin' to the music
But the livin' with the music
Like gettin' it on with Marvin Gaye
Like turnin' off the lights with Teddy Pendergrass
Like stayin' together with Al Green
Like waitin' and actin' silly with Deniece Williams
Like singin' a song for you with Donny Hathaway
Like callin' your name with Switch
Like lovin' the sunshine with Roy Ayers
Like lovin' you with Minnie Riperton
Like takin' a midnight train to Georgia with Gladys

Like bein' taken there by the Staple Singers
Like movin' on up with Curtis Mayfield
Like gettin' your car washed by Rose Royce
And wishin' on a star while you wait
Like . . . add your memory
Remember your livin' room
Remember your wardrobe
Remember your favorite movies
Remember the music you lived with
And . . . if you're not old enough to remember
Find someone who is and
Tap in, and get in, and be in, and chill in, and feel in
And dig in . . . the seventies
Yeah, dig in y'all . . . diamond in the back, sunroof top
Diggin' the scene with a gangsta lean . . . oooooh
Remember . . .

Q's on Cue

(For Quincy Jones)

In
        To
A cylindrical tube
Of brass
                Q blew
Out
        Came
Rhythmical visions
Of Music
C-O-N-N-E-C-T-I-N-G
                Me-and-You
                Q blew
                        and we grew
And
Listen
                Up!
Q's still blowin'
                        Up!
Quintessentially
Qualified
                In his
Quantum
Qwest
                To
Quickly
Quench
                Our
Qualms

Quarrels and
Quandaries
Q's on cue
            Blowin'
            Flowin'
Always showin'
                Up!
To let
The good times
            Roll
                In!

The Eternal Dancers

(For Earth, Wind & Fire)

With your love and with your lovin'
You've taught us that we can do all n all that the
Universe will allow
You've taught us that
We can sing a song . . . for you or for we
That we can get you into our lives
That we can remember . . . 21st night . . . September
That we can fan the fire
That we can tell the story of mornin' glory
All 'bout the serpentine fire
Oh yeah, oh yeah, oh yeah
You've shown us that
We can know the reasons that we're here
That we can be shining stars no matter who we are
That we can dance in boogie wonderland . . .
Or in a land called fantasy
That we can groove on Saturday night
Or that we can just groove tonight
And share the spice of life
Yeah . . . you've taught and shown us so much
And you've given us so much hope
You've let us know that
We can have devotion . . . can I get a right on
That we can have happy feelings
That we can get away
That we can be ever wonderful
And that we can keep our heads to the sky
Even after the love is gone

'Cause as long as we have you
The love will never really be gone
'Cause we can't hide love
'Cause love goes on . . . on and on
That's the way of the world

Wisdom

Everybody's droppin' knowledge these days
But is anybody catchin' it?
Seems to me that folks don't need to be droppin'
Knowledge anyway
Seems to me that folks need to be grabbin'
As much knowledge as they can get their hands on
Seems to me that folks need to
Dance with knowledge
Play dominoes and spades with knowledge
Eat collard greens and corn bread with knowledge
Make love with knowledge
Cry with knowledge
Laugh with knowledge
Breathe with knowledge
Dream with knowledge
Feel with knowledge
And become one with knowledge
And instead of droppin' knowledge
We can call this
Holdin' knowledge
And after holdin' knowledge for a little while
After groovin' with knowledge
Slappin' bones with knowledge
Grubbin' with knowledge
And after just kickin' it with knowledge
We will become one with knowledge
And we will become knowledge
And we will fly into the universe with
WISDOM

It's Okay

It's okay
It's okay to increase the peace
An' to release the peace
An' to cease the non-peace
It's okay
It's okay to let peace be still
An' to be still with peace
An' to be peaceful
An' . . . peace, y'all
Okay
It's okay to throw away
Your 9s, your 22s, your 38s, your 45s, your 357s
An' any other numbers of death you may possess
Or that may possess you
Okay
It's okay to resolve your conflicts
By talkin'/by rappin'/by dancin'
Or just by laughin'
It's okay to be smart
Intelligent and filled with knowledge
It's okay to go to lectures
Watch documentaries
Chill in libraries
And read books that don't have pictures in them
Okay
It's okay to even know that okay
Is an okay word that comes straight from Africa
It's okay to know that okay
Is the same as the Wolof
Waw kay

⊘ **DERRICK I. M. GILBERT (A.K.A. D-KNOWLEDGE)**

Or the Mandingo
O-ke
Or the Fula
'Eeyi kay
It's all okay
And it's okay to know it's all okay
Okay
It's not actin' white
Or actin' bourgee
Or bein' a nerd
It's bein' Malcolm/Martin/Maya
And as one T-shirt says
It's bein' me
Which is to say
It's bein' the true African you
And it's okay to be the true African you
It's phat
It's dope
It's flavor
It's butter
It's all of that
And more of that
And that's all okay
So go ahead and be the
Peaceful/smart/intelligent/filled with knowledge
True African you
'Cause it's okay
OKAY

Just Bein'

To be or not to be?
Now that ain't a question that too many Black folks be askin'
'Cause to be or not to be
Shoot
We already know that we be
Now most people know that we be
But they be lettin' the Tom Brokaws and Dan Rathers tell them what we
So they be thinkin' that we be illin', we be killin', we be stealin', we be
runnin', we be slippin', we be frontin', we be mackin', we be slappin',
we be hidin,' we be drinkin', we be sniffin', we be trippin', and that we
just ain't happenin'
But we are, have always been, and always will be what's happenin'
Like we be bold, we be strong, we be lovin', we be caring, we be
laughin', we be helpin', we be strugglin', we be fightin', we be
changin', we be learnin', and we be soaring
And we just be so damn happenin'
And damn
So many of us just don't know
And we should
'Cause we be so bad
Like when we be
We be bebopin', we be lindy hoppin', we be hip hopin', we be beat
boxin', we be yes y'allin', we be dance hallin', we be break dancin',
we be slidin', we be flippin', we be tappin', and we just be groovin'
'Cause we be giggin' for ares, y'all
We be doin' it all
Like when we be inventin'
We be inventin' stoplights, and lightbulbs, and moon buggies, and
blood plasma, and tennis shoes, and peanut butter, and . . . I think we
had something to do with strawberry jelly, too

Like when we be leadin'
We be great like Ramses, Tiye, Hatshepsat, Nzinga, Hannibal, Shaka,
L'Ouverture, Turner, Vesey, Prosser, Tubman, Truth, Douglas, DuBois,
Garvey, Nkrumah, Cabral, Ture, Fanon, Rodney, Biko, Winnie, Besse,
X, King, Carmichael, Newton, Davis, Hammer, Shakur, and
My ma-mamma . . . and my auntie . . . and my grand-daddy
And you . . . and you . . . and we
Yeah, we be great, y'all
Like when we be creatin' art like Robert S. Duncanson, Henry O.
Tanner, Edmonia Lewis, Archibald Motely, Romare Bearden, Jacob
Lawrence, Charles White, Elizabeth Catlett, Faith Ringgold, and Ernie
Barnes
Like we be dancin' like Mr. BoJangles, Eugene Jackson, Jenni LeGon,
Katherine Dunham, Pearl Primus, the Nicolas Brothers, Arthur Mitchell,
Alvin Ailey, Judith Jamison, Debbie Allen, Michael Peters, and Michael
Jackson
Like we be writin' . . . like Zora Neale Hurston, Paul Laurence Dunbar,
Sonia Sanchez, Richard Wright, Ralph Ellison, Gwendolyn Brooks,
George Wolfe, Terri McMillan, Toni Morrison, Alice Walker, Claude
Brown, Ernest Gaines, Henry Dumas, Margaret Walker, Nikki Giovanni,
Sterling Brown, Langston Hughes, Claude McKay, Ntozake Shange,
August Wilson, and Maya Angelou
Like we be makin' music . . . like Duke Ellington, Dizzy Gillespie, Charlie
Parker, Billie Holliday, Sarah Vaughn, Ella Fitzgerald, John Coltrane,
Muddy Waters, Fats Domino, Jackie Wilson, Marvin Gaye, Aretha
Franklin, Curtis Mayfield, Al Green, Minnie Ripperton, Quincy Jones,
Ray Charles, Roberta Flack, Leontyne Price, Kathleen Battle, Miles Davis,
Betty Carter, Bob Marley, Black Uhuru, Prince, Barry White, Luther
Vandross, Anita Baker, Sade, Stevie Wonder, Natalie Cole, Nat King
Cole, Run DMC, Public Enemy, KRS-One, Ice-Cube, Vinx, James Brown
. . . and damn . . . this could take the rest of the poem
Yeah, we be makin' music, y'all
We be so UGH in whatever we do
Like when we be cookin', like when we be playin' ball, like when we be

tellin' stories, like when we be shakin' hands, like when we be doin' our
hair, like when we be makin' love, like when we be readin' poetry, and
like when we just be bein'
We be so bad, y'all
We be everything I say and so much more
We be more than just one person could know
We be more than even we can know
We be all the be and all the we and all the we that we can be
So we don't be askin' no quasi-intellectual, pseudo-deep question 'bout
To be or not to be
'Cause we be too busy
Just bein'

Wholly Rhythmic

In zigzagging
Apartment
Wigwagging
On drinks named
After carnation-toned lingerie
(Pink panties . . . come on, now)
Heterlogging with
Five liquorice lipped
Poetically hopping over hip
Ancestrally dipped
Knights of Leimert Park
I here hear
The natty goateed
Hole in right jeans knee
Leather-coated armory
Prince of village renaissance
Valiantly decree
Africans/Diasporeans
Heretofore and before
Are extra celestially connected
To God/Jah/Buddha/Krishna/Ra/Allah
Because "we"
Inherently have
More rhythm
Than any other
Terrestrial entities
(Aha)
Reason being:
Rhythm is God
God is rhythm

More rhythm
More collision
With divine fission
(Ooh . . . la/la)
Strange syllogism
Ethnic surrealism
Afroessentialism
(Da/ha/ha/ha . . .)
Meanwhile
Back of my mind
I pigeon tiptoed along this
Self-esteemed
High conscious
Identity beam
With three-ring precision
Until this point
Blank face
Zoned out
Tuned in to
Mental key of life
Wondering

> *How much melanin*
> *Must one possess*
> *To be a blessed-by-birth*
> *Isn't she lovely*
> *Onyx deity . . .*

> > Getting dizzy
> > With Gaye sadness
> > Pondering

> > > *What's going on*
> > > *With those*

Vibrationless Africasions
Who
On an occasion
Leave skid/get rid of them marks
On after the dance floors—
Brother, brother
Are they exceptions to the
Racial rule pool
Makes me wanna double holler

Godly spirit reigns
Through all skin stains
Godly spirit reigns
Through all skin stains
Nobody's pigmently profane
And though I remain sane
Wielding my
Social fact of Blackness
From time to rhyme
I'm only sublime
Yielding to beat of humanness
Meter of openness
Lilt of togetherness
For when my face rests
With mindful breaths
My spirit listens
And I discover
If your pulse ticks
You're wholly rhythmic

Miracle

Headline:
Another Church Burned!
Triple K Membership Increases Threefold!
Anti-Jewish/Anti-Muslim/Anti-Immigrant/Anti-Everybody Sentiments on
the Rise!
Another King Is Beaten!
Another X Is Marked!
Another Riot Has Occurred!

But
Stop the stress
Or . . . what do they say
Stop the press

Let's turn off the 5 o'clock/6 o'clock/7 o'clock bad news
Let's shred the no-good-news newspapers
Let's gag/mute/and shut up the talk/talk/talk
(What are you talking about?)
Talk shows
Let's stop the stress and the press
And tune into the twenty-four-hour miracle network

And
At the top of our news . . .
A rainbow has been reported on the playground
That's right
There's a rainbow of children
Runnin'/swingin'/jumpin'/climbin'/and just havin' fun together
And the only race they know
Requires them to run

And to run fast (Tag, you're it!)
And there's harmony flowin' in their games
And it's a beautiful thing
And it's a miracle
It's a miracle

And
Our sources have revealed that
Two people have just climbed in love
He's lavender, she's turquoise
She's maroon, he's teal
He has polka dots, she has stripes
Or she's blue and he's blue too
Or he's a he
And she's a she
And it's all cool
'Cause they're in love
Not in fever
Not in fashion
Two just in love
And your eyes may frown
But
Hey
LOVE HAPPENS!
And
When it does
It's a miracle
It's a miracle

And
This just in
Two old men meet on a young park bench
And feed pigeons
And watch kids play

But mostly they share each other's memories
And it doesn't really matter that
One man's Black and before the other's white
Or that thirty years
The Black man couldn't even pick up trash in this park
What matters is they're friends
And there's pigeons to feed
And children to watch
And it's a miracle
It's a miracle

And
We interrupt this poem to let you know
You are exquisite
You are a rainbow
And that Love Happens
And that life is
Quite magically
A waterfall of miracles

Afterword

by Derrick I. M. Gilbert

Whenever I am asked the vexing question "What do you do?" my mental blackboard quickly fills with an array of titles: sociologist, teacher, performer, and, most prominently on this makeshift list, entertainer. But while cogitating on my motley existence, I realize my lips have already spoken my identity: "I am a poet." Instinctively, I declare this moniker because it most broadly encompasses what I do—listen, observe, meditate, play, and eventually celebrate life with words. But even as a poet, I have been known by different names, my most common alias being D-Knowledge. I have titled my first volume of poetry *HennaMan*, which includes pieces written between 1993 and 1999. However, HennaMan should not be construed as my new *nom de plume*; instead, it should be viewed as a concept that best summarizes a chapter of my life.

In *HennaMan* readers can examine the poetic terrain I have thus far covered, but without any authorial guidance. Apart from specific instances, which I touch on in this afterword, my poems are not organized in any particular manner: there exists no chronological ordering, no stamped dates of completion, and no footnotes indicating a piece was written for, say, an audio CD or a TV appearance. At this point I will discuss the organization of the "little ones." Grouped into four unusually titled sections, they are: Vitiligo; Blues, Blushes, Brushes, and Bruises of Blunted Love; Cornucopia of Culturally Colored Commentary; and Rainbow Transfusions.

Vitiligo

I faintly recall watching a Barbara Walters special over a decade ago featuring the enigmatic yet uniquely charismatic Michael Jackson. While viewing their dialogue, I observed that Mr. Thriller resembled a larger-than-life porcelain doll—complete with a homogenized-milk complexion, a pinched nose, and a straight processed hairdo. I adjusted the remote-controlled settings, but technology could not bring the number-one Jackson back in focus. "Damn, Mike," I hollered. Then, in a fortunate moment of TV-guided coincidence, Barbara questioned the sunglassed icon about allegations of his having undergone extensive cosmetic surgery as well as receiving sundry skin-lightening treatments. "Good one," I whispered to Barb, and then froze in anticipation of MJ's comeback. Although my memory tracking is somewhat off, I recall the King of Pop admitting to minimal facial alterations. What I visualize more clearly, though, is his body and soul language as he categorically rejected all claims of having irradiated his pigment. Rather, he spoke of his never-ending battle with vitiligo—the skin disorder that manifests itself in white patches all over the body. Apparently, Michael's case was so acute that the malady had moonwalked over his entire fragile—but of course agile—physique. "Come on, Mike," I continued, "why you telling all those little white-glove lies?"

As the segment segued to commercial, I turned off the stupefying machine and attempted to psychoanalyze the most famous man alive. How did this scary, burned-curl black cat get so off track? I then noticed my reflection in the blackened nineteen-inch screen and heard the man in the makeshift mirror yell: "Forget about Michael Jackson; you have your own blemishes to deal with!" In this epiphanous moment I was diagnosed with a lifelong case of "racial vitiligo"—an ailment that has blotched and blurred my coming-of-age. Whether it was being called "nigger" as a one-of-my-kind kindergartner, or "Oreo cookie" as a non-bused-in elementary student, or "Black Nationalist" in my college days, race has always shadowed my existence. But, alas, I am not alone—as we are all infected with this freakish virus. Racial vitiligo is a ubiquitous social epidemic that discolors all of our lives in varying degrees.

At the same time I am also aware of the prevailing wisdom of the ambiguous "powers that be," which tell us of a declining significance of race in the U.S. of A. Of course there are vestiges of past discrimination, but we essentially live in an egalitarian, color-blind society—or so they say. In my day-to-day interactions, this belief results in nonblack friends and associates making statements such as, "Look at your success, Derrick. Things have definitely gotten better for your people." Paradoxically, the "things-have-gotten-so-much-better" sentiment has engendered civil-rights setbacks—perhaps most notably in the systematic dismantling of affirmative action programs throughout the country. And, sure, in terms of some politically Ping-Ponged measures, things are better. For example, if we create pie charts displaying the expansion of the celebrated Black middle class, backed with first-person quotes and anecdotes from carefully selected representatives of this nouvelle bourgeoisie, black life is swell. Or, if we offer statistics of black success in the NBA, black achievement is gargantuan.

Irrespective of class, gender, sexual orientation, disability, or any other social classification, race sullies the lives of all Africans (still waiting to be plurally named) American. In fact, the R-word adversely affects everyone in this country—regardless of (. . . well,) race. Nor do we need to juggle numbers to sustain this claim, because we each have volumes of indicting evidence stashed in our private memory closets. Roll call! Who has ever stereotyped another person based on skin color, facial features, hair texture, or any other physical characteristic? Who has asked another human, "What are you? Are you mixed? Do you have any such-and-such in you?" Please step forward, and bring with you anyone who has ever whispered, shouted, or simply thought of a racial epithet. (Take your time—there's plenty of room in these margins.) I willingly admit my part in spreading this disease; however, I am also aware of the surreptitious forces that have cunningly tossed me an abundance of diseased blankets.

The poems in this section are my way of demonstrating that— yes, Professor West—race matters. Admittedly, my early poems on the subject tend to emphasize the black/black/black (say it real fast) side of things. These poems may be viewed as the black-over-white spots, symptomatic of my morbid condition; they symbolize my pursuit of black essentialism—a true-blue blackness. When I review my writing from this identity-flipping period, I am baffled by my exclusive use of nonpersonal subject matter; I am startled by my ancestral name-dropping; and I am rueful about my posturing as a poetic know-it-all. I am most regretful, though, for having been a poetically hip hypocrite. In my valiant attempts to vindicate "blackness," I voyeuristically reified race. Ironically, my identity depended on the very construct I sought to destroy. I was thus a pop poetry doctor transmitting the disease for which I so eloquently professed to possess the remedy. Of course, I offer this as a broad-stroke critique of my work, knowing it does not apply equally to all the poems in this section. All of these poems, for instance, show my great interest in the flexibility of language, while the newer work explores my "oh, that's who I am" inner self. Perhaps my shift is best marked by the creation of the namesake poem of this book. Written throughout 1998, while concurrently trying to complete my dissertation, "HennaMan" signals my unequivocal acceptance and appreciation for the full spectrum of humanity. I now use my pen to connect dots rather than create more of them.

Blues, Blushes, Brushes, and Bruises of Blunted Love

This section was initially designed to exhibit my love poetry. But after reviewing a boxful of unorganized pads and loose papers, all I found were self-absorbed abstracts on the theme, my "what be love" scrawls, calligraphic scribbles of transitory carnal encounters, my feeble efforts of testing the shallow waters of erotica, and a biting babble of blighted romance—what poet Gerry Quickly might call my "bitter ex-girlfriend" poems. But I was unable to identify work I felt comfortable calling "love poetry." Instead, I uncovered assorted flavors of blues, blushes, brushes, and bruises of blunted love. I hypothesized that my dearth of heart-pumped writings was caused by my lack of experience in the area—that is, I had never "fallen in love." However, a quick retrospect of my life with verse revealed this thesis to be spurious. (Flashback!)

When I received my first poetry anthology in a ninth-grade English class, I instinctively searched the pages for romantic passages—even as a child, I was intrigued by the notion of giving oneself to another. My own infatuations, which dated back to a six-year, young captivation with a girl named Karen, had sadly been stymied by my lack of confidence and eloquence. Nor was I impressed with the grade-school Casanovas who seemed to manipulate words to tempt girls; their approach lacked the honesty and gentleness I so desired. Perhaps this is why I was most moved by the words of mostly "dead white men" who elegantly spoke of surrendering themselves to another. Wow! I envied their courage while simultaneously dismissing it as a phenomenon of the textbook past.

In the tenth grade, I "fell in like" with a classmate named Lisa, whose old-spirit beauty nurtured my immature imagination. But, again, in spite of my intense enchantment with this high-school angel, I never had the courage to even say "I—I—I kind of like, like you." In a moment of mind-stuttering desperation, I called Lisa's best friend, Tina, to ask for some advice. After boo-hooing with me about my timidity and my tongue-tiedness, Tina guilefully inquired, "Derrick, don't you like reading poetry?" Before I could answer, she continued, "If you're having such a hard time talking to Lisa, why not write her a poem?"

Although I adored reading poetry, I never knew I had permission to participate in the doing of it. What a revelation! I now felt my soul revving up for the green writing light. After hanging up the phone, I wrote Tina a poem entitled "Think Mellow," about her favorite color—yellow. Zoom! I then wrote Lisa-inspired poems throughout the night. Unfortunately, my pen-stroked feelings did not win Lisa's affection; but this not-so-quickly crushed crush did initiate another relationship—with "my girl" Poetry. Since I daringly displayed my newfound love, I soon acquired a reputation for being "the poet." In fact, I was frequently asked by "homies" to "hook them up" with chivalrous words for their own Lisas. Alas, I was Millikan High School's (love) poet-in-residence.

As I transitioned to college, I continued writing enraptured poems. However, during freshman year I became a born-again Nubian Black Man ("you know what I'm saying?")—listening to X-Clan; adorning myself in red, black, and green Africa medallions; donning "By Any Means Necessary" T-shirts; and proudly proclaiming the Black Man as the original man. My cultural nationalism was complemented by a fervent intellectual immersion, in which I began absorbing as much information as I could possibly borrow, check out, steal, or even buy (if I absolutely had to). I subsequently found myself having the loudest voice in classrooms, study groups, protests, and dining halls. Then, at the start of sophomore year, a comrade named Tim Hood bestowed a nickname on me that would eventually become my alter ego. I recently called Tim, and asked him to recount his creation of my a.k.a.

"You don't remember?" he said. "It was when you were living up in the Afro House with Defari. One night you had just finished typing a paper on one of the computers they had. And, you know, back then most of the brothers were writing like five- or six-page papers, but (damn) you had those twenty-page epics with footnotes and everything. And you were always reading—like all the time—and you remembered the stuff you read. So I just always thought you had a little more passion for learning, for writing, for reading, for talking, for all of it. It was like you were doing the knowledge. And, you know, your name is Derrick and we already called you 'D,' so it was like 'D' doing the knowledge. That night it just collapsed into D-Knowledge. And I don't remember calling you Derrick ever since."

During my D-Knowledge transformation, I turned my attention away from writing poetry. Occasionally, I would sneak in a seduction poem; but my energy was directed toward studying theoretical texts, writing critical essays, and throwing my multipitched voice into Berkeley's cacophonous winds. Yet my interest in poetry never waned—I continued reading verse and I regularly attended local readings (though never participating). I fondly remember first witnessing the goddess gentleness in the words of a college-blossoming Ruth Forman; and I also remember being inspired by the presence of the humble, brilliant, committed, and always giggling June Jordan. Poets and poetry were all around me—but poetry was not coming out of me.

As I discussed in the introduction to *Catch the Fire!!!*, an anthology of African-American poetry I edited in 1998, I did not recapture the poetic Holy Ghost until entering graduate school in 1993. And as I have mentioned here, my first poems were contrived for claps and laughs. During this indefatigable period, I did not write much love poetry; I felt the topic lacked the punch necessary to knock out the crowd. At another bizarre extreme, I believed amorous poems alienated the "fellas." I reasoned that men preferred not to hear "mushy stuff"; and I chose not to be labeled "soft" or "sprung." On those rare occasions I did attempt to write "love poems," I made sure my work was emotionally safe. Sometimes I achieved this by evoking the erotic, while other times I created male-privileged "I spite you" poems. "Against Common Sense" and "Salvation" are two examples of the latter. And though I apologize for the cruel-spirited nature of these works, I still feel obligated to include them here; their omission would be a denial of my past.

I am delighted to say, however, these are poems of yesterday. Today I am pleased to announce the on-time arrival of my solar-system mate, who stimulates my growth and rocket-fuels my imagination. With divine sign language, she shows me that "all poetry is love poetry." Mom! Guess what? I am in love—from head to belly button to stubbed toe. I have spirit-connected with a woman at peace with life, with change, with growth, with conjoining. I have been blessed with a sun-prancing seraph who spits fire on my defects, and who enlightens me about the cosmic meaning of "burn, baby, burn." Tabbatha, you are my inflamed bliss, and I will always sear with you. That's the truth.

Cornucopia of Culturally Colored Commentary

A few years ago *60 Minutes* blab man Andy Rooney made some less-than-sensitive comments about Native Americans. Specifically, the rancorous Rooney suggested that protests over the appropriation of tribal names for sports teams was "silly," and that "American Indians have more important problems to worry about." On another occasion, the often-loony Rooney crooned that Native American casinos only produced "piles of cash for sleezeball owners."

Not surprisingly, Rooney's remarks generated considerable outrage—with some Native American organizations and leaders calling for CBS to fire the broadcast veteran. I, too, was perturbed by the comments of a man who probably learned "Indian History" by watching the Lone Ranger.

I then fantasized about Rooney getting the network ax, and the producers of *60 Minutes* asking me to be his replacement. But instead of dispensing random quips about "this and that" (à la Rooney), I would contractually recite poetry on various topics. For my inaugural address, I envisioned delivering "Why I Would Never Buy a Jeep Cherokee" as a direct rebuttal to my predecessor's ignorant psychobabble. If this chimera had somehow materialized before 1996, I would have indubitably drawn from the poems in this section, for they constitute the bulk of work created during my D-Knowledge schizophrenia. These are the poems I spoke of earlier that cater to audience whims. Some of them were even written for a particular project and therefore don't have an organic genesis.

This is surely the case with the diligently didactic "Higher Learning," which was "produced" for John Singleton's film of the same title. These "commentary poems" were conceived and executed with the explicit goal of "edutaining"—to use a term coined by the venerated rapper KRS-1. To achieve this end, I made sure my writing proceeded in linear fashion so that people would not get lost in unguided images; I included catchy hooks to ensure that audiences would remember my poems; and I used satire and humor to demonstrate that we can "lightly" deal with "heavy" issues.

Eventually, though, I grew tired of the somewhat formulaic nature of my work. Even when addressing a range of issues, my poems began feeling the same to me. Moreover, there was no me in my poetry. Nevertheless, I cherish these "D-personalized" poems, and I have fond memories of performing them throughout the country. In fact, I still recite many of them, for they are fun to deliver and receive. And, hey, in these overly prescribed Prozac and Saint-

John's-wort days, "fun" is spirit therapy. So happy reading, y'all! Who knows—maybe our paths will cross at the intersection of the next sixty minutes?

Rainbow Transfusions

In April of 1999 I visited San Quentin prison, which ironically sits on a scenic Bay Area peninsula north of Marin and adjacent to the Richmond Bridge. Josh, a dynamic and compassionate graduate student in U.C. Berkeley's department of sociology, had invited me to speak to a storytelling class he'd been a teaching assistant for at the prison. Although I accepted the invitation without hesitation, I was somewhat nervous about the prospect of intimately interacting with fifteen inmates. I remember asking myself: "What if they think I'm too wordy? Too nerdy? Too privileged? Too removed from their reality?" To diminish my apprehensions, I resigned myself to "just keepin' it real," which led to a profound soul-connecting session. These literature aficionados showered me with questions, answers, ideas, and excitement. Not long into the meeting, the "fellas" were sharing their poetry. Without exception, their work was characterized by an addictive optimism that left me high off being human.

The following evening I ventured to a poetry reading in Berkeley. I was still peaking from the previous night, but I was craving another word fix. Midway through the event, I was bewildered by the nonstop moans of despair. Every poem I heard was filled with rage, and sometimes hate. That relatively privileged individuals articulated these emotions further perplexed me. After all, twenty-four hours earlier I witnessed incarcerated men—many of them "lifers"—uniformly celebrate the positive dimensions of life. "Why aren't these poets doing the same?" I asked myself. By no means am I implying that poets should dispense with vitriolic, venting vexations; however, I am suggesting that we never allow gloom to override our creations. Even when commenting on grave problems, we must be motivated by utopian ideals. It is time we write away our wounds and start pen-pumping new visions into our hearts. The poems in this concluding section are celebratory, nostalgic, and full of hope; they are my way of transfusing rainbows into our drained veins. And though these poems primarily extol the joys of the so-called black experience, they are dedicated to all humanity. That's the key idea anyway: seeing/feeling/being the universal in the specific. At the risk of sounding trite, I will posit that the ecumenical thread that will inevitably bind us is love.

HennaMan thus concludes with a poem entitled "Miracle," which is my "love vision" just waiting to be launched into actuality. Ladies and gentlemen, boys and girls, the countdown has begun. (10-9-8) We will soon depart from this earthly malaise. (7-6-5) Light-speed traveling to a "hueless" human world. (4-3-2) Landing on Planet Henna—where many become (1). Blast off!